Sit & Solve

CRYPTOGRAMS

National Puzzlers League

Sterling Publishing Co., Inc.
New York

2 4 6 8 10 9 7 5 3

Published by Sterling Publishing Co., Inc.
387 Park Avenue South, New York, N.Y. 10016
Includes material previously published
under the title *Hard-to-Solve Cryptograms*
© 2001, 2004 by National Puzzlers' League
Distributed in Canada by Sterling Publishing
℅ Canadian Manda Group, One Atlantic Avenue, Suite 105
Toronto, Ontario, Canada M6K 3E7
Distributed in Great Britain by Chrysalis Books Group PLC,
The Chrysalis Building, Bramley Road, London W10 6SP, England
Distributed in Australia by Capricorn Link (Australia) Pty. Ltd.
P.O. Box 704, Windsor, NSW 2756, Australia

Printed in China
All rights reserved

Sterling ISBN 1-4027-1309-6

CONTENTS

INTRODUCTION
And Hints for Solving

A cryptogram is a fairly straightforward puzzle. Every letter gets changed to another letter of the alphabet. Letter substitutions remain constant in any one puzzle, but change from one puzzle to the next. These cryptograms are especially hard to solve, because the creators have taken pains to remove the easiest steps usually available to solvers. Few codes will reward you if your method of breaking a cryptogram is to try every three-letter word as a candidate for *the*. Articles, conjunctions, even prepositions have been considered weeds. (Notice, that sentence has none of them!) Few sentences may have quite the rhythms of ordinary speech. Simple phrases such as "the early bird gets the worm" may be transmogrified to something like: *Early rising avian catches earthworm, appeasing hunger. Perhaps worms should snooze longer.*

You may be wondering at this point if these puzzles can ever be solved. How would you even begin? One of the most popular methods for experienced solvers is to sort out the vowels from the consonants. Letters that only occur once or twice are most likely consonants, as are letters that make most of their appearances at the beginnings and ends of words. Letters between two consonants are usually vowels. Once you have made a start on that process, start looking for words that begin with two consonants—the second is a good candidate for H, L, or R. If many words end with the same consonant, your best bets are D, S, and T. Three consonants at the end of a word? Try *-ght* or *-tch*. Determined as they may be, constructors have trouble eliminating all prepositions; though they may have sidestepped *in* or *on*, they probably had to use *within*, *into*, *above*, or *atop* to do so. Look for likely places and patterns for these and other longer prepositions.

Lest you despair, there are also hints for each puzzle. On pages 7 through 11 are numbered instructions on how to change an encoded letter to one in plaintext. Under each cryptogram you're referred to three of these that will tell you how to decode three of the letters in your puzzle. Use them sparingly, lavishly, or not at all, as you please. There also may be a hint in the title—but keep your mind at its most flexible here. Something entitled "High Spirits" might be about some elated people; but it's even more likely that it describes ghosts in the attic or a mountaintop saloon.

These cryptograms have all originally been culled

from the pages of *The Enigma,*
the monthly magazine of the National
Puzzlers' League. Founded in 1883, the NPL is the
oldest continuously existing puzzle organization in the world.
Word puzzles of all kinds are posed by the members to each other in
The Enigma, and cryptograms are just a small part of them. Even more
puzzles are the meat of the annual convention, held in different locations
around North America every July. To read more about our history and the puzzles we do, we hope you will visit our website, www.puzzlers.org. You'll also find
there sample puzzles and information on how to join. And, in the on-line *Guide to
The Enigma,* you'll find a more in-depth article on solving cryptograms.
    One last word: the puzzle bylines, given along with the answers at the back
of the book, will probably look rather strange to you. Most members of the NPL
choose a nom de plume when they join, and it's by our noms that we know
each other. A nom can be simply a nickname or it can be arrived at through
complicated wordplay. To meet the people behind the noms, you'll have
to join the League. In the meantime, try these cryptograms and get
to know the puzzles behind the people.

1 U→R
2 A→H
3 P→S
4 C→V
5 G→F
6 B→Y
7 X→Y
8 D→E
9 Y→C
10 C→W
11 T→X
12 B→S

13 D→Q
14 X→O
15 H→O
16 U→E
17 J→U
18 D→W
19 T→U
20 N→E
21 Y→E
22 W→U
23 T→R
24 F→E
25 E→K
26 R→D
27 G→M
28 L→T
29 Y→L

30 R→H
31 T→N
32 K→Q
33 G→P
34 K→A
35 Z→Y
36 P→H
37 M→O
38 Y→O
39 A→Y
40 L→G
41 P→I
42 T→P
43 Q→N
44 Z→W
45 P→G
46 T→A

47 M→T
48 Q→R
49 V→N
50 O→Y
51 E→Q
52 K→H
53 H→U
54 W→S
55 O→I
56 N→D
57 U→M
58 D→X
59 D→Y
60 A→E
61 T→O
62 I→L
63 J→E

64 Y→V
65 N→Y
66 C→H
67 T→M
68 C→M
69 A→T
70 W→T
71 O→P
72 F→W
73 S→X
74 G→O
75 Z→T
76 Y→S
77 C→G
78 F→H
79 C→O
80 W→B

81 D→L
82 G→E
83 W→I
84 X→P
85 B→T
86 P→E
87 E→P
88 Z→O
89 C→E
90 F→R
91 F→Y
92 D→U

7

93 F→C
94 L→O
95 E→L
96 R→P
97 X→W
98 I→X
99 D→N
100 R→S
101 W→Y
102 L→E
103 X→V
104 D→O

105 J→A
106 Q→B
107 T→H
108 F→Y
109 Y→I
110 H→T
111 F→L
112 Z→N
113 R→I
114 Y→M
115 K→X
116 N→R
117 K→P
118 H→A
119 X→G
120 J→M
121 L→S

122 K→S
123 D→T
124 S→U
125 A→C
126 U→G
127 G→A
128 O→J
129 I→F
130 Q→S
131 M→Z
132 Q→K
133 A→G
134 J→D
135 A→S
136 C→Y
137 P→M
138 P→T

139 L→D
140 S→N
141 V→S
142 P→A
143 U→F
144 P→W
145 Z→I
146 I→N
147 X→B
148 B→M
149 H→I
150 S→E
151 S→P
152 M→B
153 E→T
154 X→I
155 V→Q

156 Y→P
157 B→C
158 S→V
159 A→F
160 R→Z
161 K→G
162 I→E
163 V→M
164 U→O
165 J→O
166 A→V
167 Q→E
168 Z→A
169 Y→N
170 X→R
171 X→S
172 J→S

173 F→X
174 D→H
175 O→E
176 U→D
177 K→M
178 W→O
179 C→R
180 L→U
181 I→R
182 Q→H
183 M→F
184 O→D

8

185 V→H
186 A→I
187 G→S
188 B→H
189 X→U
190 U→H
191 C→T
192 I→W
193 E→S
194 X→T
195 Q→A
196 T→I

197 Q→P
198 Y→Z
199 A→P
200 O→H
201 K→I
202 P→B
203 H→M
204 H→F
205 U→Q
206 P→U
207 P→F
208 H→W
209 A→O
210 V→P
211 Q→U
212 E→Y
213 J→F

214 T→M
215 E→H
216 G→Q
217 V→E
218 I→T
219 U→K
220 G→C
221 U→N
222 L→I
223 F→T
224 E→A
225 I→A
226 F→S
227 R→W
228 S→F
229 Y→G
230 I→S

231 D→S
232 K→T
233 K→Z
234 Z→U
235 B→I
236 J→Y
237 R→B
238 G→X
239 Q→M
240 B→O
241 H→C
242 M→K
243 A→L
244 D→G
245 J→H
246 O→N
247 M→H

248 E→R
249 C→N
250 L→C
251 O→Z
252 Z→G
253 S→L
254 G→L
255 R→U
256 H→L
257 M→P
258 S→G
259 Z→M
260 E→F
261 T→L
262 N→G
263 G→J
264 O→L

265 N→S
266 M→R
267 R→N
268 O→M
269 D→F
270 T→E
271 A→W
272 G→U
273 L→N
274 G→N
275 J→N
276 P→O

9

277 Q→L
278 D→A
279 R→Q
280 N→L
281 E→N
282 H→R
283 K→U
284 B→T
285 O→T
286 F→I
287 S→M
288 K→N

289 U→L
290 I→Y
291 N→W
292 B→E
293 E→I
294 M→C
295 K→P
296 T→D
297 C→I
298 G→T
299 T→C
300 W→C
301 I→K
302 J→T
303 T→S
304 P→J

305 L→X
306 U→S
307 P→N
308 W→V
309 O→W
310 L→H
311 O→B
312 T→J
313 L→R
314 W→D
315 P→K
316 M→Y
317 I→U
318 H→Z
319 J→W
320 Q→G
321 N→I

322 S→Y
323 H→D
324 C→A
325 V→X
326 C→Z
327 B→L
328 W→A
329 V→O
330 W→Z
331 Q→O
332 I→H
333 W→R
334 E→G
335 F→N
336 Z→S
337 R→T
338 I→Z

339 R→F
340 R→L
341 Q→T
342 N→H
343 M→S
344 E→Z
345 D→I
346 A→N
347 Z→L
348 E→D
349 Y→A
350 I→G
351 S→H
352 O→A
353 A→M
354 R→O

355 X→S
356 E→C
357 G→K
358 M→V
359 Q→W
360 T→B
361 E→W
362 X→C
363 J→R
364 L→F
365 N→O
366 F→O

10

367 D→M
368 Z→E
369 Q→I
370 O→G
371 R→J
372 I→P
373 V→A
374 T→F
375 J→B
376 S→K
377 U→X
378 K→O
379 N→T

380 X→F
381 T→W
382 B→A
383 U→V
384 V→B
385 Z→V
386 Y→X
387 I→O
388 M→N
389 V→C
390 R→E
391 H→P
392 K→L
393 F→J
394 M→U
395 X→L

396 Z→D
397 U→B
398 N→C
399 U→Y
400 D→V
401 O→R
402 W→L
403 K→Y
404 C→P
405 T→G
406 I→B
407 S→T
408 H→Q
409 V→U
410 L→J
411 B→U
412 I→C

413 R→K
414 Z→H
415 U→I
416 A→Z
417 U→T
418 K→F
419 L→A
420 J→G
421 X→D
422 V→F
423 K→C
424 B→P
425 B→N
426 N→Q
427 G→Y
428 V→I
429 X→M

430 W→K
431 R→A
432 U→W
433 K→B
434 J→L
435 C→S
436 J→I
437 G→D
438 A→L
439 H→S
440 P→C
441 E→O
442 W→H
443 S→R
444 J→D
445 U→I

446 V→W
447 O→U
448 L→O
449 E→O
450 C→U
451 W→N
452 I→S
453 F→A
454 H→G
455 E→H
456 B→T

11

1. National Security

VHCE EGZHSPJ GE JPVX GÚ IPEZQCGE

PWPSRZHTP: ZAHV ILGKPSZ HV VG VPSLPZ PTPE

DGRLV ZLRFD JGPVE'Z XEGO OAQZ AP'V JGHEC.

Hints: 141, 444, 59

2. What a Drag!

MK MW WOZS WDGW BVS UGWKEMIIK OSKBOW DBWSI

HMKQIGLK G KMPV OSGHMVP "PSBOPS FGKDMVPWBV

KUDISQQSH DSOS"?

Hints: 150, 240, 174

12

3. Any Antiques?

IJPWU IEPR IVDPEHVDR IDXG

IJKWEPJHEPN IXDRENP IJWHXDERK IVDPEKQRZ

IJYXDEHR IDRPWQ IAJH.

Hints: 129, 14, 307

4. Hoover Says...

QCFSR CTP CF CAVERN XTTPRXRNXQAP CNNTCZNXEF WET

NDCN PAPVPFN EW EBT REZXPNI JDXZD RPPSR BFPCTFPY

VEFPI.

Hints: 174, 23, 441

13

5. Woody Allen Quote

X'L GMC Y AUDI EMMO ODXAUD ... MGTU

X CDXUO LYNXGE Y V-CVDG YGO JMVGO VW

QWUZZXGE YGCXOXQUQCYKZXQSLUGCYDXYGXQL.

Hints: 409, 274, 184

6. Senior Citizen's Complaint

JHQCKAIC T WQTHH CJGD J LCKQKIPJLCTN XDXKPR, QCD

VTHX LPKGTUDU YKFJUJRW TW KV ZADWQTKYJEHD

ZAJHTQR!

Hints: 54, 256, 429

7. Wishbone of Contention?

LIEIPNTGNR ETXDB BGVWIPH YNCIM YTGIM

VFGVWIR YTNRVFGHI OGPF P-HFGTPH HNJGRE "OI MX

VFGVWIR TGEFPH."

Hints: 138, 309, 14

8. Change to Morgue?

DROGCEQRVPDOHQ ECBLM MLCMBCE GLAQ RPHDOQCG RIUL

HIB DVPKOMLM OQ SPIGM VLECBL OQHLGA CAQLV

ROB. JICEMCVF!

Hints: 341, 159, 254

15

9. A Cut
Beneath Him?

KLENB FLGI YLEF-OBIICIFX OVNB RETB SLK PEN

OLECG VDWHFVHPCK PHCQ HN EXVDJ FVGVDJ

CHOD RLOIF.

Hints: 188, 162, 309

10. Overgrown

KPG RXI AJJ BWGIWEZ JAM HGYMK UXI UGZYE AEG NPGE

PGM FXFXSUGM IYIIAAK UGFYSG NYIGMSGTAE-KWVGB.

Hints: 93, 397, 209

11. Taking the Fifth

VWOX OX QJ YAMOJQAB JRFOXW XJVJU, ZLV

Q UAVQOJ FVVA YG VW QFCWQZV WQX ZJ YHOVVM

PAB VOH OV QCCQAX.

Hints: 55, 171, 275

12. Above Reproach?

KDHOHKHUZ HU UTZSONHVF ONYO MTB KYV SYUHPM YCTHG

... QM GTHVF VTONHVF, UYMHVF VTONHVF, YVG QSHVF

VTONHVF.

Hints: 49, 149, 423

13. Temptation

GR NMWWTF-FECZFUJ ZBMJPFUC, ZBF

GEJEJE, JXZ ZBF EQQTF, BEC GFFJ HMWFTR BFTW

ZX GF ZBF DXUGMWWFJ DUAMZ.

Hints: 275, 224, 261

14. Good Advice

QM OB ZQMRDC QVHQBM RDVG OL, ICLLGDO ICDO

YPECAMRQRYDPM DI NCYOL YM EDPRYNADAM RD

CLERYRAGL.

Hints: 268, 129, 337

18

15. Try T-F!

YALE LEGIT OMNI YLY KVUHHIF RUGBLVG

KVMJCF PVG WLVJX TLG EUTX OVGF GL YLY

KVIFGULT GL UTMCLAMGM.

Hints: 32, 156, 298

16. Anyone Disagree?

SMGWWG EG PGHKFHWAYHMX SJXCKZHCGE: "MC MX QJC

QGAGXXHWT CJ KQEGWXCHQE CYMQOX MQ JWEGW CJ

HWOKG HPJKC CYGF."

Hints: 171, 125, 333

17. Self-Defeating

FORGET INDIAN WOE MN AGCN MSXEGET

HDUE LDSX DUE FDSYN RD TNR XGH DB O XOR,

FOXXL NZNXYDE BDYHGWC XNZGEHY SY.

Hints: 337, 20, 405

18. Say Thaw?

EYE CAT QUIP IMATH HQU ECBVULYZ INOABHYZ RQA QIE

YOBADOYI? QU'E VYU IRISU IH OYNQH RAOEUPYON YJ

HQUPU RIB I EAN.

Hints: 348, 110, 227

19. Brunch Is Better

ANWHC FPKJ MBF JHWZX IHXZ DJKHX
VKHGN, AJBC DUBENO. BNJPAHGO WNX ZNBJX
XZKRYHCW. IZNC MPCN, GUHRA ABGE HCXP ANM.

Hints: 414, 382, 192

20. Rainer Thought

NFRYT QNJWT: "RJKT MJHOFOWO FH WXFO, WXLW WQJ
OJRFWVSTO CNJWTMW LHS WJVMX LHS INTTW
TLMX JWXTN."

Hints: 70, 270, 359

21. Comforting Statistic

WYYGNPVHO BG BUL DWBVYWH, GJB GS LDLNA

BUGJIWHP QLGQCL RUG ILLZ WH LTGNYVIB, GHCA SVDL

WNL NLWCCA QGIILIILP.

Hints: 400, 228, 102

22. Hello and Goodbye

BHK DBFMVAVJNJ DFBXJFT QNNJFMN: "XENEMN QHIQWN

AEXJ DHJQNVFJ—EL ZBM MRJ QFFEXQH, MRJ

KJDQFMVFJ."

Hints: 63, 265, 409

23. Feathered Friend

YHER TEAAGT NYXAQUY DQTZQD EMOIAE,

UXHPT GHMONMOU, UZNT OHPPZI PF UZOIHXDZ.

H VAEW HOI YMT DAOZN HXZ TAAO GHXNZI.

Hints: 118, 170, 202

24. Fundamental Identity

BCOD NSARCPCNSB AP DMIMHRMF VB BCOD VOKNMD

PZAQUMDP, CD RHQU ZSMDMCT. AL CZSMD JCDFP, BCOD

DMHD MLF AP BCO.

Hints: 447, 79, 351

23

25. Animal Crackers

DANGER OR ILL: PGON POTZGNE GFD.

UDFO BLDATE ZAD. XSYS TDMXE BOYX. KWAQ PDZE

LXOUS. XGGUGN ZLGE MDMXLL.

Hints: 448, 294, 82

26. Here, Kitty!

ULQLSFWL, QMRRAS XLFC WAZW PS ELFCUF EAUFASZ PR

SLQCU RPX RCEASC RCQLECU; FAZCX, XPNDO KXPJC

KPKMELX RPX QLECU.

Hints: 339, 95, 140

27. Etiquette Alfresco

GRACEFUL XQZ HU JUFKUE NAFJO QO

YAGLAGJ AL ORU RBYU ORQO ORUZ DACC ORUL TB

YCQZ AL ORU YBAJBL AKZ. —XAJJ XQLLUFJ

Hints: 186, 273, 16

28. Change in the Weather

IKU'D JUSOIKUJNG NR ROA XUEJARUIXUN JD HKODJUM

UKNOAX NR AXNKWJKNX JU SRAAXUCROD,

HKNKHWGDIJH TKGD.

Hints: 241, 379, 436

25

29. Keep Up the
Good Work

NSMQRV MRVRIU, IECTB PSVN FQUVEMUCBR

KVSGX MSKRMQRV, RIMUCBEIQEDK PEVIM DGD-

XVSXQRM SVKUDEHUMESD.

Hints: 272, 84, 161

30. By Georges!

BEKPXERXNA HIZTIPNE IB HREZNJ BDJAP SN FDGG JNYNE

SRYN XDZN XI BDJDPS BRZIKP ITNER PDJHN SN DP

BIENYNE UDMNX.

Hints: 387, 431, 248

26

31. What? Me Worry?

IDKBP IXCDYNPBO MNQFAXU KSCPV KWCJ WKNJC

ANKI LPIUCTKS. YPCNJ XFWKVQCJ TCIKAP VQNWKS

KWQVA ANQFD.

Hints: 297, 134, 116

32. In a Lighter Vein

RCWNZTW GWK KZFFAMDR SA SUD UAKEHSWT OZKS TWKS

SZDKRWI: UHK EUIKHNHWM GWMSDR W YTAAR NAZMS.

Hints: 26, 290, 407

33. To Start the Day

UYBFWVJ FKR QKWFR UYRRV:

"ABGRFWGRA W'ZR DRTWRZRN IA GIVX IA AWS

WGMBAAWDTR FKWVJA DRPBCR DCRIEPIAF."

Hints: 205, 385, 135

34. The Price of Progress

WNCMQG AQNCETM WKQLMF FKLMU TQMCHF TKQCU ZNQ

AKXWMGF. MKTI TEUFNWMQ GND KULMC "AKAMQ NQ

APKUFHT?" FDHTM.

Hints: 199, 48, 299

35. Bad Stuff

QZBJGZUOJMC YZEOC, EPGA, ZUJB QZJV,

AZQFZAC, DNSGQGUZQFGVE, COUCOCQZ: AQGEE

VZOJGVZN TQGBSUOE.

Hints: 89, 285, 193

36. Who's Hue

PMH YAUACQ KCHHV, OHUUAX, BVG EUFH TBO EH

QOVAVOTQ ZAC DVHSWHCDHVYHG, YAXBCGUO, BVG

THUBVYMAUO, CHQWHYPDIHUO.

Hints: 382, 9, 179

37. Riddle.
(Are You Nuts?)

VD FTL PMJW HWJWA RVATAH VA TAW PMAI

MAI WVUPN VA NPW TNPWZ, OPMN IT FTL PMJW?

M IVDDWZWAEW TD M RVATA.

Hints: 61, 346, 96

38. Dry Humor?

BSVRSJKQKIMTJ XSSJT, UHMPWQF OSLT XKVJMPMGZ.

JBSMV EGJBVKKX JKOSQT GVS SXEVKMLSVSL

OMJB "BMTT" GZL "BSGVTS."

Hints: 188, 150, 127

39. For Driving
After Dark

YGRMI KVUEMB JCPTFMB, VJPYA GYIS KBOPIIM

QBPCPYA, BMOWJ, "PN SGV TOY BMOW CZPJ, SGV

OBM VE CGG TIGJM."

Hints: 74, 41, 169

40. Oxymoron, or Censored Opinion?

"MG YIMSZ GMQOCZIH GMQOC YIMSZ, PKL GMIZ GMQOCZIH

GMQOC GMIZH, BOPC LV 'GIZZLVS GMQOCZIH' MQOC?"

—QZVIQZ YPIUMK

Hints: 5, 320, 200

41. Good Answer

FBTKWBC FH KPTZZ HX FWCBB-IBTC-
HPUZ: "MX IBZFBCUTI LTZ LBUGBZUTI, LWTF
MZ FHUTI?" CBZNHGZB: "FHQHCCHL!"

Hints: 176, 290, 223

42. Relatively Speaking

OR JHSVYFBD CVEFGHRU? BCHIAUNFSFIN TDZHWUD VWY
MCVED JHOFER FU CVOD, HIG ZCYFUBOHU TDZHWUD
BCDR HYDI'B.

Hints: 118, 66, 95

43. Maturation

WE OIL USUALLY, AMROE'T ZNSGR NOT
PSAYLTTLR TMCL ANSDALLY ANMXTOYR USHL
NXYRDLR QSGGSYIT MY ALGLHSTSMY.

Hints: 69, 143, 169

44. Some Don't Need Any

QPHK SPEK-WMPKMK TPF AWMF QJTMJFM YJOMK UBF PZ
WHT: "DJK TPKM QJTM WMPKQ YMIUMVZ. JF JZWMIQ,
WM YBZ WPHI."

Hints: 442, 214, 335

33

45. "I Want to Go ...

... HFIE JK CL MNJJMO PQFRR RAFIE

ND EOFMFEOEBF, AFSFNN, SAOQO JAO

ABCBABCBDBEBDBEBFGBFF PK RSNCCNDP HL."

Hints: 321, 411, 33

46. Who Kneads Dough?

KFJJTBUNPJLP'T YAMJIFD RPI MJXUFT ORATF OLNFT TAUI

UAO-KDLXFI ZPDZT. YAUVT UANFI ZRF KLF DPZFT AY

KFJJ'T PMJZT.

Hints: 394, 275, 24

34

47. Road Warrior

LBSVRL IHV LUSNL HL SNOGV GEGL

KQABGV LRTIJGV SO LRHRTSO NHCSO HMGHZ: "BHLL

NTRM IHQRTSO: ZVTXGV IMGNL RSKHIIS."

Hints: 82, 121, 424

48. Such Sweet Madness

PLO YIXOZPRNZTOT EGKBOXXKG EKJGOT XMGJE KZ LNX

QGKXXFKGT EJHHCO YZT FOZP QGYHM XKCWNZS LNX

FYBBCO.

Hints: 318, 87, 72

35

49. A Change for the Worst

ABDOMINAL TDOXARAYS IMTTMXVI NY DAOUN

ONNOTH EDWRA ONNAXCNWSP NY NUOZAUIA

XMRNWTYRYUAL CROWL TOUCAN.

Hints: 379, 299, 404

50. Word Queeries

EG WEIQVJVPVW FQVA CVIIO, LYV FV "QVJVPVW" FQVA

AVLU? EG WEIKYVVU FQVA KLZUEDZI, LYV FV, EG

GDDPQLYWO, "KYVVU"?

Hints: 217, 5, 72

36

51. Too Much Talk

QAA PEL NKGAZ'W Q WPQHL QVZ UQVI KS

BW QGL WPQHLEQVZW, CBP KBG DKARPRJRQVW PLAA

BW PELGL QGL WPRAA Q AKP KS EQUW.

Hints: 438, 138, 195

52. Premature Celebrating?

CNUILK XUZIG JKI DEEZIILIS TNS VNGFDEF, AOJ PXU

JNVG "SNNHU? RNO HOUJ AI ZDGGDEF! DJ'U

BKSDUJHXU IYI."

Hints: 345, 281, 162

53. Vicious Circle

EWYWL PVEA TJVDJ GEW DHPW BVLMX.

JGT VM VX HE WQQ VM DJGDI-BSRR GB

DJGRWMXWLGR, OSX XJW LWMSRXVEQ DJVDIWE VME'X?

Hints: 320, 245, 281

54. Floral Profusion

QVLFUOQ CXQC PCCBUQ LOA TCN HUOA SDQYJQ

HYCDQXW, QLPK DUSK HCNX GQSLYW WSLFGQA

CO QLPK WUAQ.

Hints: 79, 167, 440

38

55. Front-Yard Blight

PGMV AWHF BLG QOBVIL AWHPB: XOPQ
XNZVBOI ANZFOPRHV PHM HJBPJFTGW WGZN, NOYG
ANZFOPRHV VGYGP LJPCWGC BH HPG.

Hints: 141, 412, 310

56. Ham and Wry

MV. P. OXJSHTZ'P VHZRUA UB CIUXAXQO OXIXQO C
FUVKJXVHQZ BUT C SCA KHTBUTVCQFH: "VN AHCT FRCK!
OUUA XPQ'Z ZRH MUTA!"

Hints: 163, 3, 370

57. Vintage Groaner

BAEEQ UEP ZAPPED: AM I LDZZACT ICP I
LIEM NUBOB I NDCO ICP I LIEM, YLIO PUDB I
FUIOEUIP NUKD OU? ICBYDZ: OLD PUNS.

Hints: 225, 310, 95

58. Tiptoe

UJFNVI NU EARFYNEU RQN PJCZI: "UJF FJ MIYEOSAPEFI
FXI VJYYNCJYR NU FXI XJAYR JG YIMJRI NU FXI SJJFR
JG ERVIURNJU."

Hints: 321, 100, 165

40

59. Good Question

APTDKPSZ RIPYF OAXLPN XY OAF NIQFW

KXJT: "BD OABN BN OAF ITOBLPOF MPLF, JAG PWF

OAFG QTPGBYM BO PMPBY YFHO GFPW?"

Hints: 235, 319, 261

60. Takes On Perspective

"QRIGVQHA QSKWIGHIH QS RQWIKE UWPUPWEQPS EP PSI'H

RQHEGSKI TWPA EDI UWPMVIA." —FWQEQSXH PT BPDS

XGVHFPWEDC

Hints: 276, 439, 353

41

61. ... And All
Through the Doghouse

KXCLH BXQ PES LJWFP HXOF GQXPBI

OFMSEWFQA EM ASFYU, BEPLFYOFC GYBEP MYS. ('SZYA

CFPJFC GFFM EQ LQFYAF NYAA.)

Hints: 157, 189, 44

62. No Foot Like ...

QAWGZXW RTLGYZ IFY ZWGULGQ UBWKK; QAWGZJW KWLZ

IFYC JLQFI IYWUF FLK TBZ ZTQK KTJY GYV IALUEK.

Hints: 328, 120, 78

63. Heavy Misapprehension

UPQ VDPO LTF QPVCID QJDZIPFB IJB WRJUHDTU

LTF VDB GJBVB. VDB ZFPJDTF OXBD IJAP HUTQU

KVRZI JGTXD QIJRPB.

Hints: 428, 123, 105

64. Wild-Goose Chase

AWL XSN. IEH LED OR PIT OFT HAY PA DTP ITS GTP LAD

UR AN; HEP BAT! NIT NUB COG (RAP ART ASP AS

HOP), NA STY, NUL FES, IUL ROW.

Hints: 332, 139, 244

65. Cockeyed Optimist?

JFFUBA SNGYJ DK FIVOP, ANE JONKKJ OUBE

CDDQ JLVIYJ IO IB IBASF UBOD FILP—OPNJ, "FTFVE

LSDQ PIJ I JSUTFV SFIBUBA."

Hints: 172, 24, 225

66. Dropping Out

QX TQ! GE D ERQJOB XJM BUSSUHLAWE ZOUTWUTN WXUM

GQMW HQGGQT HXJOJHW O. VXJW MXQLAB U BQ?

Hints: 331, 27, 401

44

67. Making Ends Meat

VLNJ, VLBCUKBC VLGWTHF VYWAN KBGS

TKN VHHI-CFKBZKBC QYWTKBH YBZ CHGN Y UKGGUH

VHTKBZ KB TKN ESFA.

Hints: 384, 201, 77

68. Without a Seatbelt, Yet

XCOSW OIUJM MXC DTONNL VSCHQOQM NXCCV AXU CQFULN

SPWPQH UQ PQWPOQ CTCVXOQMN? ACTT, MXOM'N O YPQC

XUAWOX CAC WJC!

Hints: 271, 164, 47

69. It Happens

XYF QIYV XYF'MD KHJJAD-GSDJ VRDI XYF
RDGM "LIGB, ZMGZQAD, GIJ BYB" PDNYMD XYF SDW
WY WRD PMDGQNGLW WGPAD.

Hints: 424, 70, 127

70. Topless in Tampico

IKSMGQ, LKDVSA SQOXKBAVM KRQJX BQOX QHKSATP-
PTBBQL OQFRHTHQ, IJBTO XQ IKHN, "V BQUTN FP GKX
VS OKZZHQS, MVOMQ."

Hints: 331, 294, 34

46

71. Downhill
From Here

GYHQIDE AWDSU IDEJKG ARUSSR ZJPS YJUZS

ZDLR RG VSU YGEJY VGAIDRJY. RVSH XGN VJPS RVS

IDEJKG D.E.M.

Hints: 356, 185, 29

72. Does It Hurt?

KZ YLZ YXX WVDXUJMLW YSI UYNSJZLW, YSI MDL

TYJZLNYX NW MDL MKS BXZWC YSI FXMMI YSI FMSZW.

—JCMLZYD

Hints: 349, 92, 313

47

73. Vocal Advice?

UP UT WILD OIHEGXH PR LIBF IAKLDEPIF
EXQQHIT BHRXF; UP JBD CI POI CITP LITERATI
PR PIHIEORAI TBHITEILTRAT.

Hints: 162, 415, 256

74. Where's Smokey?

ICGUYCDD IXUCDZ IMUC IMTFZCUD IUCNHCQZYA
IXHQO IUMTFZCQCO IGHQG IYCCMQT IUXK
IYMJBCUMQT IYGKCD.

Hints: 129, 29, 231

48

75. Needs to Be Resolved

ABCDEFG AHBIDJFGJ IKLIBE AFDMJ

CDGFIDE MDC IOFMIDGI IKHDIBCEIJ JFNFCD FD BPI

NHBQPI RHNFGFMIJ.

Hints: 324, 99, 159

76. Grid Lock

BICK ZAPS HOGI FLDK YOGI BAPD DIOM CEXI TOMB

SEDI. DINK FSOT: ULHI HOED GOBI PUID ZOYJ

CSIP AXIM SICK REBI.

Hints: 144, 99, 253

77. Revenge! (Maybe...)

PRE YJA RLA WNO UCH. KLA WCO LIO FCO

SFQ LJQ LIA PCI UCO PKE BLE LON DNN WLK. UFE

IFD RLP SLO GLO DRF XLE HNO BLE FIN ALE.

Hints: 212, 3, 20

78. Old Saw

FPR XEXYTJTGWA JXYZRCFRY PGZRH FG AXER FXS IGCRL

QL VGYBTCU WCHRY FPR FXQMR, QWF TC FPR

RCH PR UGF CXTMRH.

Hints: 390, 22, 323

50

79. Killer Cryptogram

MDR CODY DJKW BH WJKYBK LWYZJC.

FZGDJZ MDR KWH KJM, "BKAYAMDOAWNDRC

KZYWKZWH!" CDEZDHZ ZQCZ MZQQC, "YAWJ CAZ FQDLC!"

Hints: 363, 328, 2

80. Recess

TSIVWQ-RVLR BNPXRNQ TSQM-QVLLNH TSILUN LMO

AWQ TSYNIVUNJ. TSLLUVIL, TSOZ QWZN, TSTVBJS

PUJW WAANQNH.

Hints: 312, 124, 40

 51

81. Don't Call Us ...

EPVQFLLPW AKLKTPV BOQAOQQPB

YFEPMSW KEEWOGKLJ KMJPV PROLT GSVVOGSWSA

IOJKP CVOJJPL COJY AKSIP GVKRFL.

Hints: 353, 124, 220

82. Soap Opera

YW KLEWZA, O.R. IHHKAL'R SERIAL CHAR HW MBYWX;

UHAR BEOWULF YW LYDAL. KHBXR IAEL COF SELMBA,

"Y'G SLYWCYW' YW VIA RAYWA ..."

Hints: 451, 313, 100

83. Just a Coincidence

ZCA, D BITV GRC NTHHTICAG MDPAG YIO

WYAG IYHCA TI CYPGR, KFG RTV HYIZ ECTEWC RYSC

ZTF HCG IYHCO HTRYHHCO NRYIQ?

Hints: 203, 398, 30

84. Less Filling

RGNXTS GRGAZBAXZ VPU AXC ZBAJP QVAX GOPXT OVAZVAY

VP DBJQZA'P FGNX XABJYL ZBJYL PB GIBVZ YBVAY VA

PLX LBQX.

Hints: 138, 346, 396

85. Pleh!

FKNTWHVQHXO TECCSQ OPGFHZEOHPZ
OZQWHQB TWSXGBZPNQF FTQOXAXOWSSK APZ
BKFSQYXO FPSMQZF.

Hints: 253, 326, 386

86. Timeless Philosophy

OM DAVITEOY XIANXI DONKEY QAEYSM ARS, "SCI TOW
OPSIN SAVANNAH EM SCI SCENT TOW AP SCI NIMS AP
WARN KEPI."

Hints: 209, 116, 407

54

87. Mudslinging

EUROBONDS SHJOHDIC HER FAIB
EDRIAFCNPBE KZNBAR NZ YBHKB WHNYXHNBA, WHWU
CZNXDNYRNHCEDCI.

Hints: 80, 379, 249

88. Monstrous!

"JOZLI" LISRV IGWEF "FCZLI." "TJAGW" FUJIOV "VJKFL
OILYF." "RMSY-VMNF" DWAFV AMHQIB IPZFL "GMY" ISH
IPWLF "YMISZ." XWQ KFIDXB!

Hints: 225, 178, 17

 55

89. Consuming Passions

LETTUCES WPD ODPIUTA P.Y.E. SUYO GEZDIUOR
LBDX BRIR: RSCDX JELEIDTU, BREWLBRRYR,
SEWQGUTARIY, ETW TEZRS DIETARY.

Hints: 206, 390, 188

90. The Site of Blood

DEP UZIH UZHD IZCKNJD CZTWHANI TCNJIX TIP DPCAIUZ.
MEZI XNITHAIU V IZUTHAKZ, WETG FTJUED MENFZ
MTP HN VTIY.

Hints: 46, 186, 146

56

91. Still Going Strong

CARTOON LAD, WHITEJOY ATPR LRWHN

RNZAP FHTG GOHNL ZHEM, ERTPATIOL

ZNRHYEHLPATU LADPOOT-ZAP-CON-LOERTY ATXR.

Hints: 354, 186, 58

92. A Royal Pain in the Castle

VEEM DILLY LUTHOFLSK. BKL NIBS ALLU SKOS BKL

KOB BIAALMLC NEML SKOY KLM BKOML EA

FOC KLTM CORB.

Hints: 52, 441, 13

93. No More Tangles

BZURDBVHD ARUXHWVS KALJG QLAVN

JBDC NRWWSVN UABHEVG ESBZQBHK DAVGGVG:

EXDG CVA CRBA RHN CVA SLGGVG.

Hints: 56, 330, 187

94. No Sweat!

RKX CUCXHAVC, KWC TFJQ RCTTKB PKLLCN OAV ECEKXQ,

PMEICN DK HKWHTMVAKWV, FWN TCD OAV AEFLAWFDAKW

XMW BATN.

Hints: 378, 451, 170

58

95. Un-Funny Bone

STU BWIXTES TSOTILSX EI BCLFB ES

ZITBACK-UHMTR ZCEEI, PITHYB WFFTI HIQ.

(SEO CHWXALSX HPEWO AWQTIWB BLOWHOLES.)

Hints: 140, 119, 441

96. Vow of Poverty?

ZYX WYVUTUSRQ SWPYW QSRTON NS MSZLYWN

QKSIYQAJZ. TWSRK HSVPYP RKSZ HJUVUZT NS

NRWZ KWSKOYN.

Hints: 379, 255, 112

97. Mercury Left Behind

FYI WHY JHPF FWHQ, ZPFYI, JHPF AYIGQ; ZY
WHY SYHY PI YWHXS. XSLQ KYLIE QP, ZSP EYXQ XP
CHLAY PGH QWXGHI XPCWM?

Hints: 146, 21, 282

98. Sheltered Life

SHOTGUN, KZWTPYRN GRAZE RGX MZUGNL-TWIN-NGH
NHRSLIHUE. NHMGLE BZRG YN PHJGR LZ HWW YR
LGRLN, HRK TZUTZYNGN.

Hints: 82, 118, 265

99. Alphabet Oops!

XYZ? PYXWDTDZXPZOW KANSNTH

YWLGSWOOWD USZARG AO RATIO KW GINDO END

YZOANYZS XHGSWMAUG ZGGNUAZOANY.

Hints: 433, 365, 285

100. Distinctive Quantifications

XABCYABCZABCFEUDAL CZ ZCHOP-GWELOX RWOA CR BEZCK.

XARYAKUZPSSUQSA CZ BAOLCKUS SCRA WG ASADAR

ZPSSUQSAZ.

Hints: 148, 297, 336

101. Sole Men

LIRQVJIE FQ FG JGMUWEV ZRGFEQJIP
JGARPJO QVJWI SIWOFP ZJFU XRRDJO HY LP QVJ
XVWY ZRGD FGO SWEV SIWFI.

Hints: 453, 156, 341

102. Thankless Job

NGIIEAC GNXAI XGDEYAU DIAAC YTFEYG. NREFA MEIAJTX
UDIWOOFAU DRIGWOR SITXYRAU, MAFEXA SGWXCU CGNX
FTCCAI.

Hints: 30, 370, 181

103. To Shrink Canvas

XY ZB QDJLQQXYV PQDKZ, X HFFMDP HXMD

K CDSDD KYP CODY K NXVNKZ. ZB SUBJOXKCQXUC

ELPVDP X NKU ELUC CNF CDYCU.

Hints: 8, 291, 154

104. Inelastic Demand

YNWJSIN IQN QSUQ OLWI LK BSESAU, RN OXAALI

QXEN KXSBNY IL ALISON QLR SI WISBB CNTXSAW

WL JLJDBXC.

Hints: 94, 227, 20

105. Danse Macabre

JUDY "NZTYL WZTYL" HZRWZOYM EUCY
GKFYMDUTYM IUF DXRY AXDN HZVVXK. NY WGD NXO
JYVD VZZD XK ... IGD LZG TKZA DNY MYOD.

Hints: 342, 88, 422

106. Can You Dig It?

DVP LOUAKNKXFJU EOOLFVX KZJFYFDV KA XVOFJJ
JLOTFQOVJ FV UCO ZDUCAKKQ QBJU CDGO AKTEJ FV CFJ
CODY.

Hints: 66, 286, 119

64

107. Ironic, Isn't It?

UHDCFBRZEBH QJHDH: QJESHJSIT ETESAHA

FIDM-ETERBHA GSERD—RZZHAREBHFN ZRQKCIBHQ

UNBLEMISHED BLHISHZ.

Hints: 259, 113, 130

108. Coined Phrase

FEJKDQDFEXYQ TED ZXKJXAX VEBCUX JQ JCXAJGBZKX EBAX

QXKHDS EBH GD HXBK TJGE AXCHJCU SBVEJCXQ.

Hints: 130, 104, 215

 65

109. Bankruptcy Blues

ACH, ORBIRKRE, HEKYE DSEGH

TCZRKRYCSA CPRHYH—NQBSTNRTC. FGHY CPEURKC

FEKGEBA DBCTRY DEBT HYEYCUCKYH.

Hints: 39, 393, 288

110. Down and Out?

CUZXMBFKHLNJOW CMBYK DWUSCJK (COZBXK ZCSRHNYK)

ZLNDEK ANJKLUXVBM KHCUYLOXSB. YHBMXAKCZOW,

AEBAR ZLNSABM.

Hints: 264, 101, 324

111. Look on the Bright Side

CBMYFKHIZBW UMC FBBOKCH SAZSUBZYKFZ

UKFYBMWF FKHC, XSCFPEZF SAZKUKFZ, DIS AYBFXYKQBF

YSFB-XSESYBW HEMFFBF.

Hints: 226, 201, 249

112. Last Words

JMQVK JACK VEC ZMJ ECBCEECQ JM VX QCDCVXCQ FTJ VX

CWCDJEMCZDCIAVWMNEVIARDVWWK DAVWWCZNCQ.

Hints: 302, 403, 373

113. Frank Query

TED EDGRDL LNVWEPD KR JL BIG IRK

ARMY EZL JRYK RUKLD YRWA PD VETXEMLY RU KLD

EDA CODY PD VETXEMLY RU LPMIK?

Hints: 99, 427, 354

114. Black Thumb

YENBOIL YV XK PVJCATNEIYC SOS IVY PANT YPAX LGVH—

YPAK ENN HOYPAGAS HPAI ECBAS YV CYEGY TEKOIL

GAIY.

Hints: 224, 55, 36

68

115. Crime Doesn't Pay

PTR YQLNR TBZRL PB ZKHG BC PTR FSPG
IBVWRVX' MHXRMHKK PRHU MQP IHX WRZP BC PTR
MRCFT DBV VRDQXSCN PB XPRHK MHXRX.

Hints: 240, 152, 392

116. Doctor's Orders

MHCHISOUISUO, KLAAHOBG DUBBHA URUG ALISON FEESDH
QFLIK, BHEC KSNO KUGSON, "JUDY KQFICBG. KSC.
KCUG."

Hints: 122, 191, 262

117. Take a Bow

MYJYRZRZ MDYXAZXVW MZYRZCCZSN
MVDQNDSYRXV; MVDBYMC MZXUZRVCC MDNSMAVW
MZIIZXYAN MTEXUZRJ.

Hints: 257, 145, 435

118. Double Stops?

MJLAM SOY DBLQCZEJL FSGJ XAZJOZCSQ TJLIJL CO
ARRCOI. OJD UATXSOV DCQQ TSHJ LJXLAYBUZCGJ
ALISON.

Hints: 246, 209, 350

70

119. Murder Ahoy!

WCKUZ EXBLCYKP VORP DXBE EHPUXON
HICKSON CYPKA DPBNZ UAKQHT, EXOY WHYO QHNRAO
UHCFXP UCARNKP.

Hints: 361, 169, 138

120. Mission Accomplished?

RXPZQPLW BCXWT VNHKBCWNMGD SNCG SMGPZPMN FCNQD
FPBT VCLOJLBPCLMZ DHLBMU KNJDJLBD OJUMBPCXD
CRDBMVZJD.

Hints: 72, 85, 377

 71

121. The King's English

FAURE ERSCVFM IB SPOZZOPROBE' LAOBFV,
ERBSRBS "AIUF ZF VFBMFPAD" OBM "DIG OPFB'V
OBDVCRBS HGV O CIGBM MIS."

Hints: 438, 383, 425

122. Transmission Problem

YES HEAR FLIP YUNPO SEJBN PUNK QNTBROS ECHOS TMS
TBVOJ MSODBNLP TEQO BJOE: "EAA JBTFP
YNTPBJOSOJ."

Hints: 243, 413, 443

123. Bad Signs

NOW BCNOWE DOC ALISON OWE FCIZS

QWLH UCZ UDWLEKZS GIZKUOWQ OKB XF DLUOKZS

OKU OLZQU DKNO UCLG.

Hints: 200, 18, 306

124. Portapuppies

JACK VZR WGZMM WZBBLCM JLXA BAQMQ QDMZM, VZR HCX

WZBBQDMZM, FZHM XAQX EZBF RD EZG CQMV

XGQKMDZGX.

Hints: 2, 194, 327

 73

125. Alpine Hurdle

ALISON LISAW ST FNZTJSXX LXQXNO MND ST DJA ZQB NC NDJAW LISAWL QTF ZQL URLD QT NELDQPXA QXARDSQT.

Hints: 60, 195, 365

126. Incredible!

MONKEYS GUTSYAMI TOUMB HYKK NT IXACTS YVME NKOAC BEKT YV IYL DEVMBI, PTM YVQYMTI MHE-PTOU IXNIAUYGMYEVI.

Hints: 441, 109, 392

127. Crime and Punishment?

KBDOXGEH GQDOK JUTV TED SDUKTE GK ZOXXDQ

SXOHGOUGKV. KBDOXGEH JUTV VOEW GK FETPE OK

UDKDOUZM.

Hints: 122, 454, 163

128. Some Things Never Change

OQGIBDSQ EJDCQJ PKYC OGMQ OGI HKS XFPZFYDSV CODY

GXCKGB FSQ: "QYXGZQI BQFZGJI NQBDQMQI

YZFCCQI."

Hints: 200, 76, 167

129. The Ides of April

COWKR BYIB SKIBY IRS BILKZ INK

VKNBIOR, AK ZYDPJS GK KLBNKQKJF CNIBKUPJ

BYIB DRJF DRK OZ IR IRRPIJ KWKRB!

Hints: 267, 85, 104

130. Four-Star Service

UQCL QL MKCBUWXNQXL JBZVW: "ZJV YWXZZVLQLC BY

KLEVPRVXP RQZJ SWVXUKPV QU ZJV GBD BY ZJV

FJXHDVPHXQE."

Hints: 217, 369, 77

131. Ho! Ho! Ho!

UANYOU, ENAAK ZGCYU, ISKTANVRU: UNIS
UCWNYMCL OCYG NVOCKDKVEDL YPNUGU ISNIRDKVE
ISKDMYGV GBGYLFSGYG.

Hints: 201, 334, 353

132. Late in the Day

ONE MASTER TYSASHOM ICYHUPHL: "ZXHE YWTOO WHE
CHRNE SI DTYS CNR YXTLIZY, NS WHTEY SXH YAE NY
TCIAS SI YHS."

Hints: 407, 264, 76

133. Limn Eric

CDIVCAG RAXY HUCB ZAYCDZ: "NTD
TDGXDZ SZHZAYCDZ FUG RXKEB XR DXHZ NTD FZTA
YG NXTH, GZH BTG HX YZ 'GXV PZAYCD'?"

Hints: 114, 99, 297

134. Come and Get It!

UNYRP EKPORUKPY IYOU SHGL UA ZAKRF VRW SYGHKFY
UNYJ GAKZQ OAU CHJ ZAKRF EAP RU SJ UNY
UNRPUYYOUN.

Hints: 325, 308, 347

ANSWERS

1. National Security *by SANA* Sign noticed on desk of Pentagon executive: This project is so secret even yours truly doesn't know what he's doing.

2. What a Drag! *by DOUBLE-H* Is it true that one Catskills resort hotel displays a sign reading "George Washington schlepped here"?

3. Any Antiques? *by JOPIQUIEM* Fancy fine furniture from fascinating foreign factories furnished favorite French flat.

4. Hoover Says... *by PANACHE* Banks are an almost irresistible attraction for that element of our society which seeks unearned money.

5. Woody Allen Quote *by TE-ZIR-MAN* I'm not a very good driver...once I tried making a U-turn and wound up spelling antidisestablishmentarianism.

6. Senior Citizen's Complaint *by ZYZZ* Although I still have a photographic memory, the film provided nowadays is of questionable quality!

7. Wishbone of Contention? *by ULK* Vegetarian group pickets famed fried chicken franchise with T-shirts saying "we do chicken rights."

8. Change to Morgue? *by ULK* Philanthropist named Deadman left hospital huge sum provided it would rename itself after him. Quandary!

9. A Cut Beneath Him? *by ULK* Youth rode four-wheelers with much joy but would invariably balk at using riding lawn mower.

10. Overgrown *by ULK* She put off dieting for years but began one when her cucumber tattoos became watermelon-sized.

11. Taking the Fifth *by HOT* This is an ordinary nglish sntnc, but a crtain lttr of th alphabt has bn omittd vry tim it appars.

12. Above Reproach? *by APEX DX* Criticism is something that you can easily avoid... by doing nothing, saying nothing, and being nothing.

13. Temptation *by APEX DX* Middle-Eastern thinkers, the banana, not the apple, has been widely held to be the forbidden fruit.

14. Good Advice *by RODNEY* As my pastor always told me, freedom from incrustations of grime is contiguous to rectitude.

15. Try T-F! *by ULK* Prof often gave pop quizzes without qualms but could not find guts to pop question to inamorata.

16. Anyone Disagree? *by APEX DX* Pierre de Beaumarchais postulated: "It is not necessary to understand things in order to argue about them."

17. Self-Defeating *by APEX DX* Hating people can be like burning down your own house to get rid of a rat, Harry Emerson Fosdick reminds us.

18. Say Thaw? *by WABBIT*
Did you hear about the dyslexic agnostic who had insomnia? He'd lie awake at night wondering if there was a dog.

19. Brunch Is Better *by ARACHNE* Begin your day right with fruit juice, bran flakes. Aerobics get heart thumping. When done, climb back into bed.

20. Rainer Thought *by PANACHE* Rilke wrote: "Love consists in this, that two solitudes protect and touch and greet each other."

21. Comforting Statistic *by HUDU* According to the Vatican, out of every thousand people who seek an exorcist, only five are really possessed.

22. Hello and Goodbye *by APEX DX* Old Portuguese proverb asserts: "Visits always give pleasure—if not the arrival, the departure."

23. Feathered Friend *by WABBIT* Hawk swoops through museum window, grabs painting, gets nabbed by gendarme. A fowl and his Monet are soon parted.

24. Fundamental Identity *by CORN COB* Your philosophy is revealed by your bumper stickers, or lack thereof. In other words, your rear end is you.

25. Animal Crackers *by WABBIT* Unrest at zoo: Bear badgers emu. Puma hounds gnu. Kiwi ducks hawk. Lynx bugs okapi. Keeper goes cuckoo.

26. Here, Kitty! *by APEX DX* Samantha, Muffin rate high on latest listing of names for feline females; Tiger, Rocky prove popular for males.

27. Etiquette Alfresco *by BEACON* Children may be served first at picnics in the hope that they will then go play in the poison ivy. —Miss Manners

28. Change in the Weather *by JOPIQUIEM* Man's inhumanity to our environment is causing nature to retaliate in horrendous, cataclysmic ways

29. Keep Up the Good Work *by WABBIT* Mother Teresa, Sibyl form charitable group together, establishing first nun-prophet organization.

30. By Georges! *by FRAZ* Frustrated composer of Carmen finds he will never have time to finish famous opera since he is forever Bizet.

31. What? Me Worry? *by WINDRIFT* Space shipwreck brought alien amid Mardi Gras festival. Weird humanoid visage normal among group.

32. In a Lighter Vein *by WABBIT* Dracula was summoned to the hospital just last Tuesday: his physician wanted a blood count.

33. To Start the Day *by APEX DX* Quoting the White Queen: "Sometimes I've believed as many as six impossible things before breakfast."

34. The Price of Progress *by KREMLIN* Modern produce market takes credit cards for payment. Each customer now asked "paper or plastic?" twice.

35. Bad Stuff *by RUTHLESS* Radioactive waste, smog, acid rain, garbage, fluorocarbons, etcetera: gross national products.

36. Who's Hue *by WABBIT* The colors green, yellow, and blue may be synonyms for inexperienced, cowardly, and melancholy, respectively.

37. Riddle. (Are You Nuts?) *by ADOBE* If you have seven piñons in one hand and eight in the other, what do you have? A difference of a piñon.

38. Dry Humor? *by WABBIT* Herpetologist meets, quickly weds mortician. Their bathroom towels are embroidered with "hiss" and "hearse."

39. For Driving After Dark *by ULK* Novel bumper sticker, using only Braille writing, reads, "If you can read this, you are up too close."

40. Oxymoron, or Censored Opinion? *by TE-ZIR-MAN* "If crime fighters fight crime, and fire fighters fight fires, what do 'freedom fighters' fight?"
—George Carlin

41. Good Answer *by KAPRY KORN* Teacher to class of three-year-olds: "If yesterday was Wednesday, what is today?" Response: "Tomorrow!"

42. Relatively Speaking *by ADOBE* My favorite holidays? Thanksgiving because our whole family is home, and Christmas because they aren't.

43. Maturation *by APEX DX* By age fifteen, today's child has witnessed some thirteen thousand five hundred killings on television.

44. Some Don't Need Any *by ADOBE* Said bald-headed man when someone poked fun at him: "God made some heads perfect. On others, He put hair."

45. "I Want to Go... *by BRILLIG* ...back to my little grass shack in Kealakekua, Hawaii, where the humuhumunukunukuapuaa go swimming by."

46. Who Kneads Dough *by WABBIT* Pennsylvania's founder had uncles whose wives sold low-priced tarts. Folks loved the pie rates of Penn's aunts.

47. Road Warrior *by TYGER* Sports car slows as owner eyes bumper sticker on station wagon ahead: "Pass with caution: Driver chews tobacco."

48. Such Sweet Madness *by QUIP* The absentminded professor poured syrup on his crossword puzzle and went crazy solving his waffle.

49. A Change for the Worst *by WABBIT* Exhausted chameleon succumbs to heart attack while attempting to traverse multicolored plaid carpet.

84

50. Word Queeries *by CORN COB* If disheveled when messy, are we "heveled" when neat? If discreet when cautious, are we, if foolhardy, "creet"?

51. Too Much Talk *by ADOBE* All the world's a stage and many of us are stagehands, but our politicians tell us there are still a lot of hams.

52. Premature Celebrating *by ULK* Joseph asked the innkeeper for lodging, but was told "Rooms? You must be kidding! It's Christmas Eve."

53. Vicious Circle *by VISITOR* Never mind which one came first. How is it an egg is chock-full of cholesterol, but the resulting chicken isn't?

54. Floral Profusion *by APEX DX* Examine Oreo cookie and you find twelve flowers, each with four petals stamped on each side.

55. Front-Yard Blight *by BRILLIG* News from the kitsch front: pink plastic flamingos now outnumber real, live flamingos seven hundred to one.

56. Ham and Wry *by CORN CO* Wm. S. Gilbert's method of avoiding giving a compliment for a bad performance: "My dear chap! Good isn't the word!"

57. Vintage Groaner *by SIOBHAN* Silly old riddle: if a herring and a half costs a cent and a half, what does a boatload come to? Answer: the dock.

58. Tiptoe *by BRILLIG*
Notice in Austrian ski lodge: "Not to perambulate the corridors in the hours of repose in the boots of ascension."

59. Good Question *by SISYPHUS* Halfback Duane Thomas on the Super Bowl: "If this is the ultimate game, why are they playing it again next year?"

60. Takes On Perspective *by APEX DX* "Idealism increases in direct proportion to one's distance from the problem." —writings of John Galsworthy

61. ...And All Through the Doghouse *by WABBIT* Pudgy cur not given yule brunch leftovers of steak, congealed bacon fat. ('Twas denied beef or grease mass.)

62. No Foot Like... *by ULK* Grandpa joined the dancing class; Grandma said they might teach his old dogs some new tricks.

63. Heavy Misapprehension *by ULK* New item for weight watchers has plankton for its basis. Its creator must have known zilch about whales.

64. Wild-Goose Chase *by XEMU* Old Mrs. Hub dug in the ice box to get her pet dog an os; but woe! She saw zip (not one ort or bit), so Rex, sad cur, had nil.

65. Cockeyed Optimist? *by WABBIT* Seeing lumps of earth, guy stuffs tiny wood scraps at an angle into each—thus, "every clod has a sliver leaning."

66. Dropping Out *by NON SEQUITUR* Oh no! My k yboard has difficulty printing this most common charact r. What should I do?

67. Making Ends Meat *by WABBIT* Busy, bungling butcher backs into his beef-grinding machine and gets a little behind in his work.

68. Without a Seatbelt, Yet *by WABBIT* Heard about the classy pregnant sheep who enjoys riding on Indian elephants? Well, that's a fine howdah ewe due!

69. It Happens *by LUV* You know you're middle-aged when you hear "snap, crackle, and pop" before you get to the breakfast table.

70. Topless in Tampico *by WABBIT* Pancho, waxing nostalgic about lost orangey-yellow sombrero, pules to pard, "I loved my hat in saffron, Cisco."

71. Downhill From Here *by DITTO* Olympic skier Picabo Street gave large gift to her local hospital. They now have the Picabo I.C.U.

72. Does It Hurt? *by SIOBHAN* We are all sculptors and painters, and our material is our own flesh and blood and bones. —Thoreau

73. Vocal Advice? *by DADA* It is very helpful to read encrypted puzzles aloud; it may be the best response to telephone salespersons.

74. Where's Smokey? *by MAYA* Fearless forest fire fighters frequently found frightened fauna fleeing from flickering flames.

75. Needs to Be Resolved
by PEN GWYN Frantic forensics expert finds ancient DNA evidence exonerates simian in Rue Morgue homicides.

76. Grid Lock *by AI* Deft bowl game punt came down near five yard line. Next play: huge gain made when back flew over left side.

77. Revenge! (Maybe ...) *by WABBIT* Shy kid had pet bug. Lad put ant out for air and sun but sly jay ate wee pal. Boy now has fat cat who may get jay one day.

78. Old Saw *by SHIMINATOR* The avaricious carpenter hoped to save tax money by working under the table, but in the end he got nailed.

79. Killer Cryptogram *by DITTO* You spot orca in arctic waters. Before you can cry, "ichthyophagous cetacean!" someone else yells, "thar she blows!"

80. Recess *by MAYA* Junior-high teacher jury-rigged jungle gym for juveniles. Juggling, jump rope, jujitsu also offered.

81. Don't Call Us... *by BLAZE* Personnel manager dismissed hopeful applicant after eying curriculum vitae written with mauve crayon.

82. Soap Opera *by WABBIT* In France, U.S. hoofer's washer goes on blink; does laundry in river. Folks hear guy warble, "I'm wringin' in the Seine ..."

88

83. Just a Coincidence *by DART* Yes, I know the commonest first and last names on earth, but how many people have you met named Mohammed Chang?

84. Less Filling *by SHIMINATOR* Bakery abandoned its new donut line after finding it couldn't make enough dough to avoid going in the hole.

85. Pleh! *by ILLUMINATOR* Sympathetic puzzle constructor created palindromes specifically for dyslexic solvers.

86. Timeless Philosophy *by TE-ZIR-MAN* As comedian George Carlin points out, "The day after tomorrow is the third day of the rest of your life."

87. Mudslinging *by CHARTS* Dyspeptic campaign ads urge disgruntled voters to heave bathwater, baby notwithstanding.

88. Monstrous! *by DADA* "Ultra" ranks above "extra." "Jumbo" equals "super large." "King-size" comes midway after "big" and afore "giant." How peachy!

89. Consuming Passions *by WABBIT* Cannibal duo touring U.S.A. list favorite chow here: elbow macaroni, headcheese, ladyfingers, and navel oranges.

90. The Site of Blood *by DART* Shy gent gets nervous reaction around any syringe. When donating B negative, chap laughs whole way to bank.

91. Still Going Strong *by R/EDS* Pioneer Six, launched into solar orbit many years back, continues broadcasting sixteen-bit-per-second info.

92. A Royal Pain in the Castle *by CORN COB* Poor Queen Elizabeth. She must feel that she has suffered more than her share of bad heir days.

93. No More Tangles *by FRAZ* Impatient Rapunzel grows bored with dazzled princes climbing tresses: cuts her hair and her losses.

94. No Sweat! *by MAYA* For exercise, one lazy fellow jogged his memory, jumped to conclusions, and let his imagination run wild.

95. Un-Funny Bone *by WABBIT* New surgeon entering OR slips on freshly-waxed floor, breaks upper arm. (Not laughing about humerus situation.)

96. Vow of Poverty? *by DART* New religious order sought to convert spokesman. Group folded upon failing to turn prophet.

97. Mercury Left Behind *by DITTO* Men are from Mars, women, from Venus; we are here on Earth. This being so, who gets to drive our Saturn today?

98. Sheltered Life *by WABBIT* Campers, dolphins enjoy new forest-plus-sea sanctuary. Safety zone is haven to all in tents, and porpoises.

90

99. Alphabet Oops! *by APEX DX* DNA? Undergraduate biology newsletter claims it might be short for National Dyslexics Association.

100. Distinctive Quantifications *by APEX DX* Hemidemisemiquaver is sixty-fourth note in music. Hendecasyllable is metrical line of eleven syllables.

101. Sole Men *by DITTO* Brothers at an English monastery enjoyed their Friday meal cooked up by the chip monk and fish friar.

102. Thankless Job *by DART* Worried owner notices treed calico. While fireman struggles through branches, feline bounds down ladder.

103. To Shrink Canvas *by DITTO* In my recurring dream, I looked like a tepee and then a wigwam. My psychiatrist judged I was just two tents.

104. Inelastic Demand *by DITTO* Despite the high cost of living, we cannot have failed to notice how it still remains so popular.

105. Danse Macabre *by DITTO* Late "Hokey Pokey" composer gave undertaker bad time with coffin. He put his left foot in ... but you know the rest.

106. Can You Dig It? *by DITTO* Any petrologist keeping obsidian or gneiss specimens in the bathroom must have rocks in his head.

107. Ironic, Isn't It? *by BARTOK* Penultimate scene: scarecrow awarded long-awaited brain—immediately misquotes Pythagorean theorem.

108. Coined Phrase *by DITTO* Philosophers who believe change is inevitable have seldom had to deal with vending machines.

109. Bankruptcy Blues *by BLOSSOM* Yes, Virginia, Santa Claus definitely exists—worldwide. Just examine January credit card statements.

110. Down and Out? *by NIGHTOWL* Ambidextrously adept gymnast (albeit bankrupt) bought customized trampoline. Predictably, check bounced.

111. Look on the Bright Side *by RASTELLI* Nearsighted man seeking optometrist misreads sign, consults optimist, who prescribes rose-colored glasses.

112. Last Words *by DITTO* Today they are not referred to as deceased but as electroencephalographically challenged.

113. Frank Query *by DITTO* Can anyone explain to me why hot dogs are most often sold in packages of ten and buns in packages of eight?

114. Black Thumb *by LANX* Talking to my houseplants did not help them grow—they all withered when asked to start paying rent.

115. Crime Doesn't Pay *by ILLUMINATOR* The judge hoped to play on the city workers' baseball team but was kept on the bench for refusing to steal bases.

116. Doctor's Orders *by DITTO* Veterinarian, suddenly called away during office hours, left sign saying, "Back shortly. Sit. Stay."

117. Take a Bow *by BARTOK* Paganini practiced pianissimo performance; perhaps pickiness prompted pizzicato plucking.

118. Double Stops? *by DITTO* Xerox and Wurlitzer have potential merger in offing. New company will make reproductive organs.

119. Murder Ahoy! *by NIGHTOWL* Juicy whodunit kept show watcher aquiver until story climax, when Jane Marple caught culprit.

120. Mission Accomplished? *by DANDR* Building tough cryptograms from familiar words with conventional syntax presents vexatious obstacles.

121. The King's English *by WAMPAHOOFUS* Elvis sighted on grammarians' planet, singing "Love Me Tenderly" and "You Aren't Anything but a Hound Dog."

122. Transmission Problem *by KRAY* Car Talk guys chose radio show moniker after NPR nixed previous name idea: "All Dings Considered."

123. Bad Signs *by DITTO*
The mother who caught her young deaf son swearing punished him by washing his hands with soap.

124. Portapuppies *by DITTO* When you cross collies with Lhasa apsos, you get collapsos, dogs that fold up for easy transport.

125. Alpine Hurdle *by DITTO* Eskimo skier in downhill slalom got in the way of other skiers and was just an obstacle Aleutian.

126. Incredible! *by TYGER* Tabloid predicts earth will be sucked into black hole in six months, yet invites two-year subscriptions.

127. Crime and Punishment? *by DITTO* Stealing ideas from one person is called plagiarism. Stealing from many is known as research.

128. Some Things Never Change *by DITTO* Headline writer must have had fun composing this actual one: "Escaped leopard believed spotted."

128. The Ides of April *by LANX* Given that death and taxes are certain, we should be extremely grateful that only one is an annual event!

130. Four-Star Service *by BRILLIG* Sign in Yugoslavian hotel: "The flattening of underwear with pleasure is the job of the chambermaid."

131. Ho! Ho! Ho! *by AV* Smurfs, Gummi Bears, Chipmunks: such Saturday fare unfailingly rouses chuckling children everywhere.

94

132. Late in the Day *by APEX*
DX Lin Yutang astutely observed: "When small men begin to cast big shadows, it means the sun is about to set."

133. Limn Eric *by ULK* Their furniture went back to Louis XIV because they could not pay Louis for it by the thirteenth.

134. Come and Get It! *by ULK* Inquiry from this ermine: "Can anyone determine why folks of note can wear my coat, yet say to me 'you vermin'?"

PUZZLE NUMBERS

95

96